CAREERS IN THE
HOMICIDE UNIT

CAREERS IN THE
HOMICIDE UNIT

CORONA BREZINA

ROSEN
PUBLISHING®

New York

Published in 2014 by The Rosen Publishing Group, Inc.
29 East 21st Street, New York, NY 10010

Library of Congress Cataloging-in-Publication Data

Brezina, Corona.
Careers in the homicide unit/Corona Brezina.—First edition.
    pages cm.—(Extreme law enforcement)
Includes bibliographical references and index.
Audience: Grade 7 to 12.
ISBN 978-1-4777-1710-3
1. Police—Vocational guidance—Juvenile literature. 2. Homicide
investigation—Juvenile literature. I. Title.
HV7922.B74 2014
63.25'952023—dc23

                                                          2013011261

Manufactured in the United States of America

CPSIA Compliance Information: Batch #W14YA: For further information, contact Rosen Publishing, New York, New York,
at 1-800-237-9932.

CONTENTS

INTRODUCTION

Many criminal cases have been declared "the crime of the century!" by the media. The 1924 murder of Robert Franks committed by Leopold and Loeb. The 1932 kidnapping and murder of Charles and Anne Lindbergh's baby. The 1994 O. J. Simpson case, which involved the murders of Nicole Brown Simpson and her friend Ronald Goldman, and which became known as "the trial of the century." Then there are the criminals whose very names induce shudders: John Wayne Gacy. Charles Manson. Jeffrey Dahmer. The Son of Sam.

All these cases involved homicides. Murder, more than any other crime, rivets the public attention. Sometimes the public spectacle camouflages the terrible hurt and sense of loss occurring behind the headlines. The grieving family and friends of a murder victim just want answers that will give them a sense of closure. They want justice for the victim who was lost.

Homicide detectives are the investigators charged with solving murder cases. They respond to the crime scenes where violent or unexplained deaths have occurred. Sometimes they may have to pass by news trucks and crowds of gawkers. Other times, they may arrive at a desolate scene in the dead of night where the only other people in sight are crime scene investigators and fellow officers. No

Crime scene technicians preserve evidence at the site of a shooting. Markers indicate the location of each piece of evidence, which will be photographed and recorded.

matter the circumstances, homicide detectives must be ready to take charge of the case.

The homicide unit is the most elite detective squad in a police force. Anyone interested in becoming a homicide detective must first demonstrate his or her capabilities as a officer. Then an officer may be assigned to the level of detective and, eventually, apply to the homicide unit. In some departments, achieving the rank of detective qualifies as a promotion. In others, it is considered a lateral transfer—an assignment with different duties but no change in formal rank or pay. Unlike patrol officers, detectives wear plain clothes, maintaining a professional appearance at all times. Homicide detectives generally work with a partner.

If you're interested in pursuing a career in the homicide unit, you should first determine if the field of law enforcement is a good match for you. Many police departments offer ride-alongs, in which citizens accompany patrol officers on their shift. Law enforcement officers find rewarding work in enforcing laws and protecting the public. Homicide detectives tend to relish the challenge of finding the killer and being able to tell the victim's family that the murderer has been caught. Nonetheless, law enforcement and detective work, especially, are demanding, stressful, and dangerous. For many homicide detectives, their work isn't just a job—it's a calling and a responsibility to murder victims, to their families, and to society.

CHAPTER ONE

OVERVIEW OF THE HOMICIDE UNIT

On the night of July 11, 2011, a passenger in a black SUV opened fire on a crowd of about twenty people in front of a house on Scheerer Avenue in Newark, New Jersey. A gunman on the porch returned fire. Eight people were shot in the exchange. A fifteen-year-old boy lay dead.

A team of nine homicide investigators responded to the incident. They belonged to the Essex County Homicide Task Force, made up of twenty-nine detectives, which had recently been formed by combining several urban homicide units. The reorganization was intended to improve the effectiveness of homicide investigations and prosecutions. Detectives on the squad worked long hours to counter a surge of violence that had left the community angry and helpless. It was the county's sixty-ninth homicide of the year.

Detective Michael DeMaio, captain of the squad, was among the homicide detectives on the scene of the Scheerer Avenue shootings. Other detectives interviewed witnesses and tagged evidence. DeMaio was particularly interested in .40 caliber shell casings found on the porch. The previous

Captain Michael DeMaio (*second from left*) and colleagues on the Essex County Homicide Task Force share evidence near the crime scene at Scheerer Avenue in Newark, New Jersey.

week, .40 caliber slugs had been taken from the body of murder victim Marquis Robinson. In addition, undercover police officers had overheard conversations indicating that the two incidents were related.

The shooter on the porch had been wounded. A trail of blood revealed that he had escaped through the backyard.

The detectives interviewed victims in the hospital who had been injured in the Scheerer shootings and checked their criminal records in the police intelligence banks. They discovered that one of the victims was what DeMaio described as an "arch-criminal," as reported by the *Star-Ledger*. Raheem Cleveland had been arrested more than a dozen times for drugs and assault charges and had been released from jail in March.

The squad's ballistics expert had been called in to examine the shell casings. At one in the morning, he reported that the same gun had been used in both the Robinson killing and the Scheerer Avenue shootings. The match backed up the theory that the drive-by shooting had been a retribution attack for the murder of Marquis Robinson. DeMaio hypothesized that Raheem Cleveland—the gunman on the porch—had been the target, and that he had left the trail of blood through the backyard after being wounded.

Detectives tracked down eyewitnesses to the Robinson murder and interviewed them again. One witness confirmed that Cleveland had been the killer. After prosecutors issued warrants for Cleveland's arrest, detectives located him on Scheerer Avenue close to the scene of the July 11 shooting. Cleveland was on crutches. He refused to answer questions and was transferred to the county jail.

One homicide case was nearly resolved, but the cycle of violence allowed the Essex County Homicide Task Force no time to rest. Within a week, detectives responded to two more murders in Newark.

The Workplace

For homicide detectives, their work is a mission, not just a job. In the aftermath of the Scheerer Avenue shootings, DeMaio worked through the night. Later in the week, during his vacation time, another big case arose that required hours of consulting on the phone with his colleagues. The nature of homicide detectives' work can take a toll on their peace of mind, but it also drives them to do their utmost to bring killers to justice.

Most homicides are investigated by city or county police departments, not federal or state agencies. There are some exceptions, such as homicides that constitute federal crimes. For example, the Federal Bureau of Investigation (FBI) looks into cases such as serial killings and murder-for-hire. The FBI also provides resources for law enforcement agencies, such as information services and specialized forensic support. Local police departments can request assistance from the FBI in investigations. Various federal, state, and local units often work jointly on a case.

The homicide squad is one specialized unit within a police force. Overall organizational structure varies from one department to another. Many departments have a Bureau of Detectives branch that specializes in criminal investigations. It consists of divisions such as homicide, armed robbery, and major assaults. Sometimes there is a further layer of structure. The homicide unit may fall within a larger division such as Violent Crimes, Robbery Homicide, or Crimes Against Persons.

Homicide squads are generally considered the most prestigious and exclusive units in a police department. Large cities have multiple squads of between ten and thirty detectives. Usually, each squad is assigned to a particular area of the city.

The New York Police Department, for example, has eight homicide squads. Some homicide squads specialize in a certain type of homicide, such as gang-related killings. The Los Angeles Police Department has a Homicide Special Section that focuses on high-profile or otherwise exceptional cases.

Police departments in smaller cities have fewer specialized divisions. Instead of having a homicide unit, they may have a major crimes division of detectives who investigate a range of serious crimes.

As demonstrated by the Newark investigation, the work environment for homicide detectives is highly varied. A homicide detective must be prepared to work at any type

A detective investigating a crime spree involving a string of robberies and two homicides charts the location of each crime on a map.

of crime scene. The investigation may require extensive legwork tracking down witnesses and following leads. The job involves plenty of desk time because a homicide detective must search for information on computer databases, review paperwork relevant to the case, and file reports. A homicide detective will also confer extensively with colleagues on aspects of the case. In addition, he or she may help a prosecutor prepare a case against a suspect and testify in court.

Two detectives display a picture of a 1946 homicide victim identified through DNA testing. DNA technology and other cutting-edge tools can provide breakthroughs on cases that go cold.

Specific working conditions vary from one police department to another. In some police departments, homicide detectives have access to high-tech crime centers that facilitate their investigations. But police departments are funded by tax dollars, and during tough economic times, their budgets shrink. Some homicide detectives have to contend with cramped workspaces and out-of-date technology.

Most homicide detectives work a standard eight-hour day, but the job often requires overtime. In addition, they may be on-call for some evenings, weekends, and holidays. If a homicide occurs, they must be ready to report to the crime scene. Workloads vary from one police department to another. Some departments have enough detectives on the squad to follow every remote lead in a case. With others, though, especially where there is a shortage of manpower or high homicide rates, a new case may take priority before older cases are wrapped up.

The Cases

Homicide detectives are charged with investigating cases of suspicious deaths. These include categories other than homicide. The details of the case built by the homicide detectives during the course of the investigation determine which offense the suspect will be charged with.

The formal definition of "homicide" is "the killing of a human being by another human being with malice aforethought." There are two broad categories of homicide: murder and manslaughter.

PROFILE: VERNON GEBERTH

Former New York Police Department homicide investigator Vernon Geberth literally wrote the book on solving murders. His *Practical Homicide Investigation: Checklist and Field Guide* is recognized as being a definitive handbook on managing a homicide crime scene.

From the beginning of his career, Geberth aimed to become a homicide detective. Unusual for the 1960s, he attended college before applying to the force. He eventually earned a bachelor's degree in business administration and two master's degrees. In addition, he graduated from the FBI National Academy, one of the world's most intense and elite police academies, in 1979. Like all rookie cops, Geberth started out on patrol. His commanders recognized his potential, though, and he began in the elite Tactical Patrol Force. He was promoted to detective within three years and worked in the street crime unit and the robbery division before being assigned to a homicide unit.

Through the course of his twenty-three years of service with the NYPD, Geberth worked his way up to precinct detective squad commander,

temporary commander of the 7th Homicide Zone in the South Bronx, commander of Bronx Homicide, and finally lieutenant-commander. He has taught criminal justice courses and served as an instructor in police training programs. Today, Geberth is a highly sought-after expert for consultation in high-profile homicide cases.

First-degree murder is a killing that is deliberate and premeditated—the perpetrator planned it in advance. Second-degree murder is a non-premeditated killing—the perpetrator assaulted the victim without planning it in advance. Voluntary manslaughter is a non-premeditated killing with mitigating circumstances, such as provocation leading to the perpetrator becoming emotionally disturbed. Involuntary manslaughter is an unintentional killing resulting from recklessness or unlawful acts. Specific statutes describing each offense vary from one state to another.

Homicide detectives also investigate deaths other than homicides. These include suicides, unexplained deaths, accidental deaths, and some natural deaths, such as when the deceased was not attended by a doctor. They may be responsible for rarer death investigations such as abuse of a corpse, purchase and sale of human organs, and illegal abortion.

In some police departments, homicide detectives also investigate other serious crimes. These may include assault and battery, kidnappings, threats of terrorism, and missing persons. In smaller departments, homicide detectives may also investigate lesser crimes.

A lead detective is assigned to direct each homicide case. He or she delegates responsibilities among the other detectives involved in the investigation. The lead detective also handles communications with personnel from other departments, such as the forensics lab, the medical examiner, and the prosecutor's office.

It's Not Like TV

Most of the people who watch cop shows on television know they don't realistically depict homicide investigations. Television is

Crime scene investigators collect samples for DNA testing after the bomb attack at the Boston Marathon in Massachusetts on April 15, 2013. Evidence from the scene helped detectives determine the series of events that took place during the commission of the crime. Three people were killed and hundreds injured by the homemade pressure cooker bombs filled with BBs, ball bearings, and sharp metal shards.

entertainment, after all, and it's been packaged for dramatic effect rather than accuracy. But pop culture elements such as police dramas and mystery novels do influence people's notions of how criminal investigations work.

Shows such as *CSI* have focused on the application of forensic science in solving crimes. Forensics provides valuable tools for homicide investigators, but forensic evidence doesn't provide the clear-cut answers in real life as it does on television. Lab tests don't provide instantaneous results. Sometimes forensic analysis of evidence simply does not yield any useful information. Also, collection of evidence is done by trained forensic technicians, not the

A pair of homicide detectives arrest a suspect charged with involuntary manslaughter. The suspect provided alcohol to a minor who subsequently fell to his death in an accident.

homicide detectives themselves, who know better than to disturb a crime scene. The evidence is too important to risk contaminating. As Detective DeMaio told a *Star-Ledger* journalist, "The scene tells the story. People lie. They lie all the time. But the evidence doesn't lie."

Murder cases on television are generally solved within the hour. The shows don't depict the routine legwork, the desk work, the paperwork, the computer work, the dead ends, and the various levels of bureaucracy required of even a straightforward case. In addition, the homicide detective isn't done with a case after the suspect has been charged with the accusation. To bring a killer to justice, the prosecutor must build a court case based on the homicide detective's work. Justice is achieved through persistence and attention to detail.

In TV shows, the murder suspect is often caught at the end of an episode—a much higher clearance rate than real life. In 2011, according to the FBI, 64.8 percent of murder offenses were cleared, which in most cases means that a suspect was arrested. Rates are lower in some cities with high rates of drug- and gang-related violence. Chicago, for example, saw a surge in its homicide rate in 2012. Mark Konkol reported on DNAinfo.com that the clearance rate for homicides in the city that year was a shockingly low 25 percent.

Rewards of the Job

The rewards of working as a homicide detective go beyond money or even a sense of accomplishment. Homicide investigators are the men and women charged with ensuring criminals pay for committing horrific crimes. Many homicide detectives view their work as a duty and feel a sense of responsibility toward victims. As DeMaio told the *Star-Ledger*, "There is no better feeling than putting handcuffs on a guy you arrested for the murder, and going to a family member of the victim and saying, 'We got [him].'"

Earnings for the job vary, depending on factors such as rank, years on the job, and geographic location. Detectives and investigators are generally the highest-paid job category in law enforcement. Many departments also provide generous benefits, such as health insurance, a retirement package, and even a clothing allowance. More information on earnings for detectives and other law enforcement occupations can be found online in the *Occupational Outlook Handbook*, which is compiled by the U.S. Bureau of Labor Statistics (www.bls.gov/ooh).

CHAPTER TWO

ASSOCIATED JOBS

On February 3, 2003, music fans were shocked by the breaking news story from California that legendary music producer Phil Spector had been arrested for the shooting death of actress Lana Clarkson. Spector had worked with legendary artists such as Elvis Presley and the Beatles. He had been highly influential in pioneering new recording techniques. But in his private life, he was known for being reclusive, eccentric, and sometimes volatile.

Details about the shooting slowly began to emerge. The previous night, Spector had been drinking heavily in a Hollywood club where Clarkson had been working as a hostess. Even though they had not been previously acquainted, she agreed to accompany him back to his mansion for a drink. Spector's chauffeur dropped them off at the back door. At about 5:00 AM, Spector emerged from the house brandishing a gun. "I think I killed somebody," Spector said. The chauffeur called 911.

Police officers arrived at the scene and found Clarkson's body slumped in a chair in the foyer. She had been killed by a gunshot wound through the roof of her mouth. Spector was standing near the body and had to be subdued with a Taser.

In September, after the investigation had been completed, a grand jury indicted Spector for Clarkson's murder. The trial, which began in 2007, was highly sensationalized by the media. The prosecution contended that Spector had forced the gun into Clarkson's mouth and shot her. The defense argued that Clarkson's death could have been a suicide. The proceedings ended with a mistrial, as the jury was unable to reach a verdict.

A retrial began in late 2008, and the prosecutor once again faced the difficulty of building a case where there had been no witnesses to the crime. The evidence from the scene was crucial. Clarkson had been shot with one of Spector's guns, which had been loaded with a rare type of bullet. A rag soaked with Clarkson's blood had been found in a washroom. Blood was found on Spector's jacket and inside his pants pocket. The gun had been found at Clarkson's left side, though she was right-handed. From an examination of the body, the medical examiner stated that he considered the death a homicide.

The prosecutor convincingly portrayed Spector as a dangerous man who had threatened women with guns in the past. He also argued that Clarkson had not shown any signs of being suicidal. Clarkson had been optimistic about her prospects and had bought several pairs of shoes the day

Phil Spector appears in court for his sentencing after being found guilty of second-degree murder in the shooting death of Lana Clarkson. He received a sentence of nineteen years to life in prison.

before she died. The chauffeur proved a solid witness regarding the events of the night. Convinced, the jury found Spector guilty of second-degree murder.

The Spector case demonstrates that homicide detectives collaborate with a range of other professionals in the justice system as they work to close a case. Forensic experts scrutinize the evidence. Medical examiners perform autopsies on bodies. Prosecutors in the district attorney's office issue warrants and take the case to the courtroom. These experts do not specialize in homicide cases—they bring their expertise to investigations of all types of crimes, from assaults to property crimes.

Forensic Investigations

Forensic science is the application of scientific methods to the field of law. Forensic scientists and technicians help investigate crimes by studying the physical evidence that might yield clues about how a crime occurred or who committed it. The field of forensics brings together a broad range of sciences and areas of specialization. The forensic science unit can be attached to either the police department or the district attorney's office.

A single crime scene can yield evidence pertinent to a variety of forensics disciplines. There may be fingerprints, pools and spatters of blood, footprints, bullet fragments, pertinent

Police remove bags of evidence from the home of a murder suspect. Officers must follow proper procedures during the collection, preservation, and transportation of evidence to maintain chain of custody.

documents, insects, and trace evidence such as hairs or glass chips. Crime scene technicians collect, label, and preserve evidence from the crime scene for later examination and analysis in the laboratory, taking precautions to avoid contaminating the scene or any piece of evidence. They also photograph and videotape the crime scene.

Many forensic scientists, also called criminalists, specialize in particular areas of investigation. Forensic chemists and trace evidence examiners perform lab tests on evidence of all kinds—stained clothing, unidentified substances, fibers, suspected drugs, body fluids, and much more—in order to learn more information about the crime. Latent print examiners analyze fingerprints, palm prints, and footprints from the crime scene and identify suspects by matching the evidence to their known prints. Toxicologists analyze blood and other body fluids for the presence of drugs, alcohol, or poisons. Bloodstain pattern analysts examine blood spatters for clues on the weapon, nature of injury, and sequence of events during the attack.

Firearms and toolmarks examiners determine if specific firearms or tools—such as screwdrivers or hammers—were used during a crime. Every firearm leaves unique markings on the bullet, and every tool leaves a distinctive mark. Firearms experts may be required to examine gunpowder residue patterns or give an opinion on a bullet's trajectory.

Education, experience, and licensing requirements for forensic technicians and forensic scientists vary greatly depending on the exact position. Entry-level technicians should

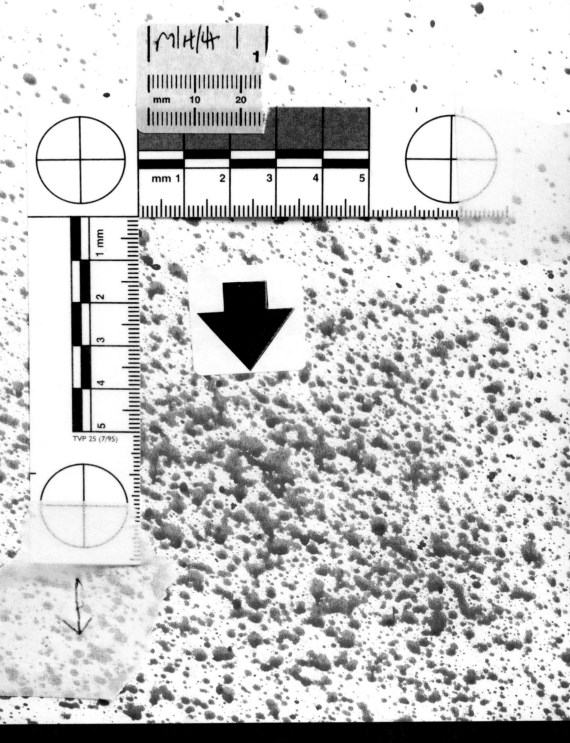

Analysis of a bloodstain pattern reveals information such as the type of weapon, the number of blows inflicted, the relative positions of attacker and victim, and the sequence of events.

have a high school diploma or GED and relevant education or training in their area. Forensics scientists generally have an advanced degree and are considered experts in their fields.

The Medical Examiner

In the case of a suspicious or unexpected death, the body is often the most important piece of evidence on the scene. Investigating the body is the duty of the medical examiner (ME). MEs are called in to investigate any death that is violent, suspicious, or unexpected. The ME also investigates any death that could potentially affect public health, such as a suspected case of tuberculosis.

Staff from the medical examiner's office prepare to transport the body of a homicide victim to the morgue, where the medical examiner will perform an autopsy.

VICTIM SERVICES UNIT

Many police departments or prosecutor's offices have a victim services unit or victim assistance unit. These groups offer support, practical assistance, and advocacy to people whose lives have been affected by crime. These individuals include the friends and families of homicide victims, as well as witnesses of violent crimes.

In some departments, especially in smaller cities, victim services units are staffed by volunteers. In larger cities, they are more likely to include a paid staff, including specialists such as victim advocates and therapists.

The family of a homicide victim is forced to make painful decisions while still emotionally distraught by the loss. Representatives from the medical examiner's office will inform them of the timetable for the release of the body and for receiving autopsy results. In some circumstances, the family may have more immediate needs. If the homicide occurred at home, for example, they may need to contact a crime scene cleanup service. If the homicide was the result of arson, the victim services unit can help arrange for temporary housing.

Victim services units provide help directly and offer referrals to other social services agencies. One of their most important services is counseling to survivors who experience lingering trauma from their loss. They also provide advocacy to help families and witnesses navigate the complicated judicial process accompanying a homicide case.

MEs are doctors who have been trained in the field of forensic pathology. Pathology is the specialty of medicine concerned with the study and diagnosis of disease and injuries. Forensic pathologists, therefore, are experts in determining how an illness or injury led to death. The ME's office has the responsibility of collecting and evaluating evidence related to the death, performing the autopsy, and reconstructing how the body received injuries. The ME submits his or her findings in an autopsy report and may later testify as a witness if a case goes to court.

When a homicide occurs, a scene investigator from the ME's office examines the body at the scene of the crime. The body is then transported to the morgue for a full autopsy. During the autopsy, the ME examines any injuries to the body and inspects it for trace evidence. He or she also removes and examines the internal organs. Once the autopsy is complete, the ME writes up his or her findings and conclusions in a report. The ME may later be called on to present evidence in court.

MEs are highly educated. They generally earn a degree in medicine and complete additional specialized training in pathology and forensic pathology. MEs are assisted by personnel such as medicolegal death investigators, autopsy technicians, and morgue attendants.

A few states employ coroners rather than medical examiners. The two titles are not interchangeable—coroners are not required to have any medical or forensic expertise.

The District Attorney

The district attorney, also called the prosecutor, initiates charges against defendants—accused criminals—and argues cases in court. The prosecutor's role is to represent the government, and thereby the people, in criminal proceedings instituted against lawbreakers. Prosecutors work on federal, state, county, and municipal levels. In large jurisdictions, they may specialize in a particular type of case. Prosecutors are elected or appointed to the job.

The prosecutor is a very powerful official. Prosecutors use their discretion in deciding whether to charge a defendant and which charges to press. The prosecutor appears at the bail hearing, presents evidence before grand juries, attends pre- and post-trial hearings, interviews witnesses, conducts investigations, and writes legal opinions. At the trial, the prosecutor must prove the defendant's guilt beyond a reasonable doubt. The judge or the jury, depending on the type of trial, decides whether or not to convict the defendant.

Prosecutors work with law enforcement agencies while preparing a case. They issue warrants and evaluate whether evidence is sufficient for pressing charges. If not, the prosecutor may request that the police investigate further to obtain more conclusive evidence.

The public tends to view prosecutors as trial lawyers bent on conviction, but that is a skewed perception of their role. The prosecutor's role is to serve justice, not merely return convictions. If the prosecutor obtains evidence that helps the

The prosecutor exhibits photographs of a fatal accident scene—a collision that killed two people—during the opening arguments of a vehicular homicide trial.

defense, he or she must turn it over to the defendant. Also, many criminal cases are resolved by plea bargaining and never go to trial.

An aspiring prosecutor must hold a law degree and pass the bar exam that qualifies the candidate to practice law. Many prosecutor's offices require that applicants have at least a year of work experience. New prosecutors often start out working in lesser positions, such as prosecuting misdemeanors, and gradually move up to higher levels. Large district attorney's offices have a specialized section focusing on homicide prosecutions.

Prosecutors are aided by assistant or deputy prosecutors, paralegals, legal assistants, researchers, and law clerks.

Civilian Positions

Most police departments employ civilians for many support positions. Forensic technicians and scientists are civilians, for example. Civilians fill a variety of administrative and technical positions.

Civilian employees work alongside sworn police officers in their duties. Dispatchers handle telephone calls from the public requesting emergency and nonemergency assistance from the police. They determine the nature of the situation and send out the appropriate unit to respond to the call. Public relations personnel help keep the public informed and educated on issues concerning public safety. Civilians oversee police departments' payrolls, budgets, computer systems, personnel, facilities, and equipment.

Civilians perform the administrative functions that keep the department running. They staff the front desks and maintain the police records and reports. Administrative personnel assist police officers and deal with the general public. Many homicide squads have an administrative assistant attached to the unit.

Education and qualifications depend on the nature of the job. Requirements for an entry-level police clerk, for example, might include basic office and computer skills. A job as a higher-level police clerk, however, could entail knowledge on laws, specialized databases, and departmental procedures. Civilian employees may be entrusted with confidential and sensitive information that must be handled with care. Civilians working in police departments are often required to pass a strict background check.

The courts also employ civilian workers. These include positions such as court reporter, court administrator, court clerk, judicial assistant, and law clerk.

CHAPTER THREE

INVESTIGATING A CASE

On the evening of December 24, 2002, Scott Peterson returned to his California home to discover that his wife, Laci, was nowhere in the house. He called Laci's mother, Sharon Rocha, to find out if Laci was with her. She wasn't. Rocha called 911 and reported her daughter missing. Police and volunteers began a search for the twenty-seven-year-old woman, who was eight months pregnant.

Laci Peterson's mother and sister had last seen her on the afternoon of December 23. Scott Peterson told detectives that Laci had been at home when he left on the morning of December 23 and that she had been getting ready to walk their dog. Later that morning, a neighbor found the dog wandering loose with a leash attached to his collar.

From the start of the investigation, detectives were puzzled by Scott Peterson's attitude and answers. He didn't appear particularly worried about his wife. He stated that he had been out fishing that morning in his boat, even though he had never been interested in fishing and didn't know much about bait or what catch was in season. It also seemed odd that he'd leave his pregnant wife alone on Christmas Eve to drive 90 miles (145 kilometers) away to go fishing.

In the ensuing days and weeks, investigators began uncovering unsettling evidence about Scott Peterson. He had been deep in debt, and he'd taken out a $250,000 life insurance policy on his wife after she became pregnant. He had only bought the boat in December. Most suspicious was the news that Peterson had recently started an affair. He'd told the woman, Amber Frey, that he was unmarried. Investigators began keeping Peterson under surveillance. They monitored

Detectives talk to Scott Peterson as they examine his truck during the early stages of the investigation. At Peterson's trial, the prosecutor charged that he transported Laci's body in the truck.

his location with vehicle tracking devices and recorded his phone calls. Police searched his house and removed evidence. On March 5, 2003, investigators announced that they considered the case a homicide.

In early April, the bodies of Laci Peterson and her unborn child washed up on a California beach. They were found close to the site where Scott Peterson claimed to have gone fishing on December 24. Police arrested Peterson on April 18. They acted partly because they were afraid that he could flee. He had dyed his hair by the time the police found him, and he was carrying his brother's passport as well as $15,000 in cash. On April 21, Peterson pleaded not guilty to two counts of murder.

A pathologist finished the autopsies on the bodies in mid-May. The identities were confirmed through DNA testing. Laci Peterson's body had been too badly decomposed to determine a cause of death.

The trial began in June 2004. Because Scott Peterson was still maintaining his innocence, and because there were no eyewitnesses to the crime, the prosecution had to produce evidence convincing enough to make the case. Any mistake would allow the defense to raise doubts about Peterson's guilt. As prosecutor Dave Harris told *People* magazine after the trial:

For us to put on a case, we have rules we have to follow, legal requirements to put evidence in: chain of custody, foundation—those steps. And if we don't put

District Attorney Dave Harris argues before the court during Scott Peterson's trial as Peterson's defense lawyer, Mark Geragos (*right*), looks on.

them in, those witnesses don't testify. So we don't get to Amber and her tapes [of phone conversations] if we don't lay foundations.

The prosecution introduced evidence from Peterson's house, such as a computer revealing that he'd researched ocean tides shortly before Laci's disappearance. They

ELUSIVE JUSTICE

In the Laci Peterson case, investigators were quickly able to identify a suspect close to Laci with a motive to kill. During the course of the investigation, they used evidence and witness testimony to build their case.

But homicide investigations generally don't proceed smoothly and don't always end with justice being carried out. In 2008, the city of Chicago saw a particularly bloody April weekend in which forty people were shot, seven of them killed. In 2010, the *Chicago Sun-Times* won a Pulitzer Prize for a follow-up series on that weekend. The reporters described the difficulties that homicide detectives encountered. In one case—a drive-by shooting—police located the car and identified a suspect. But the physical evidence wasn't adequate to make the case. Many of the witnesses wouldn't cooperate, and the key witness later became a victim of homicide. Another case was believed to be a revenge killing: the victim himself had been a killer. But nobody would name the shooter. At least two other homicide cases from that weekend also stalled because witnesses wouldn't talk. In one

case, a victim refused to name his shooter in his dying declaration.

In only one case did a suspect go to trial—a man who had killed his boss with an assault rifle. He was apprehended after a shoot-out with three police officers.

called eyewitnesses, such as a neighbor who had seen Peterson loading a bundle wrapped in a blue tarp into his boat on December 24. The jury heard from experts, such as the pathologist who stated that Laci did not give birth before her death.

In the end, the overwhelming evidence convinced the jury. Scott Peterson was convicted of two counts of murder on November 12, 2004.

At the Scene of the Crime

Homicide detectives generally are not among the initial responding officers on the scene. The Laci Peterson case, for example, began with a report of a missing person, not a homicide. Often the emergency call is handled by a dispatcher, who asks for contact information and details about the incident. The dispatcher is able to relay information to the patrol officers so that they will be prepared to take control of the situation. The patrol officers ask for backup from homicide detectives and other necessary personnel.

Once the responding officers arrive, their first responsibility is to assess the scene, documenting relevant observations. If a homicide has occurred, officers must check for signs of life in the victim. If there is an injured victim present, providing medical attention takes priority. The officers then notify command of the situation, secure the scene by roping off a perimeter with crime tape, clear people away from the scene, and detain and briefly interview witnesses. Generally, nobody touches the body or any evidence until the medical examiner and forensic technicians arrive. If the murder suspect is on the scene, a patrol officer makes the arrest. Patrol officers protect the scene until a homicide detective takes charge.

When the homicide detectives arrive, they examine the scene with meticulous care. The initial stages are critical to directing a successful investigation and, eventually, obtaining a conviction. The investigator notes details such as the time, precise location, weather conditions, and names of other people at the scene. He or she interviews the responding officer. Ideally, forensic technicians arrive quickly to process the scene. If not, detectives and officers on the scene may take photographs and work to seal the scene or protect it from the elements. An officer also photographs and monitors onlookers because murderers sometimes try to blend in with the crowd after committing the crime.

The homicide detectives set up a command post near the crime scene. Working with the forensic team, they conduct a preliminary walk-through of the scene to determine the best strategies for processing the scene. An officer keeps a log of everybody who enters or leaves the crime scene. Officers make a canvass of the neighborhood while forensic technicians photograph, measure, search, and sketch the scene and collect evidence. It is crucial that every piece of evidence be thoroughly identified and labeled so that its integrity could hold up in court. This identification process includes maintaining a chain of custody—documentation of everybody who handles the evidence. In some cases, detectives may need to obtain a search warrant to perform a complete investigation of the scene.

Once any evidence near the body has been processed, an investigator from the ME's office examines the body and the location. He or she makes a preliminary estimate of the time of death and offers possible death scenarios based on the available evidence. The investigator also gives an opinion on whether the death took place at the crime scene or the body was transported to the scene. The body is then transported to the morgue.

Meanwhile, the detectives work to establish the identity of the victim. They also interview any witnesses to the crime. In addition, one of the detectives must locate and notify the next of kin about the death.

Launching the Investigation

During the course of a criminal homicide investigation, the detective works to determine the facts behind the killing. This

Investigators obtained a search warrant and removed evidence from the Peterson house on February 19, 2003, before the case had been declared a homicide.

fact-finding involves answering the classic information-gathering questions: Who? What? When? Where? Why? How? A detective must work painstakingly to follow every lead, but he or she must also remain open-minded to consider every possible angle of the investigation.

After the crime scene has been processed, evidence is sent to the crime lab to be analyzed. At the morgue, the ME autopsies the body soon after it is brought in. In many states, a detective is required to attend the procedure. Observing the autopsy gives the detective an opportunity to question the ME about possible clues. The autopsy may yield physical evidence, such as fibers or bodily fluids, as well as information on the cause of death and circumstances of the killing. The ME does not issue a full report until he or she has received results for any labwork—such as toxicology tests—ordered on samples from the autopsy. Crime lab analyses of autopsy specimens and evidence from the scene can take days or even weeks to complete.

In some cases, the suspect is easily identified. If the death resulted from a brawl in public, for example, eyewitnesses may be able to describe the incident. If the death occurred at the victim's home, a family member on the scene might quickly confess. In other instances, the case presents a genuine mystery that must be solved through resourcefulness and diligence. Every lead must be followed up. In the Laci Peterson case, for example, detectives identified Scott Peterson as a likely suspect early on, but they also

An investigator photographs evidence from a shooting that left one person dead and two others wounded. The photographic record of a crime scene is used during the investigation and legal proceedings.

investigated sex offenders known to be in the area and followed up on phone tips.

Homicide detectives draw on a variety of tools and tactics. They interview witnesses and sometimes re-interview them upon uncovering new evidence. They may hold press conferences requesting help from the public. They canvass the neighborhood repeatedly in the hope of identifying new witnesses. The investigation may require surveillance or undercover work. A breakthrough may occur through probing the personal lives of the victim and his or her family and friends. The detectives may draw on sources of information such as computer databases, police records, online research, and police informants.

Persons of Interest

A homicide detective must be a "people person" in the sense that he or she should be able to gauge the mind-sets of people involved in the case. A detective involved in the Laci Peterson case said, "We've been doing homicides for a while. When you compare Scott's demeanor with other people we've dealt with, he didn't even register on the scale as far as seeming concerned [about Laci]," according to *People* magazine. On the job, homicide detectives find that people react to homicide in various ways. There may be distraught family members, reluctant eyewitnesses, and frightened bystanders. Depending on the attitude of the witnesses, the detective may use different techniques during interviews to draw out information.

Witness testimony can either aid or frustrate a homicide investigation. When witnesses are waiting to be interviewed at the scene of the crime, they are separated so that they will not discuss the incident and influence each other's accounts. All witnesses' testimony is double-checked for truth and accuracy. The perceptions of eyewitnesses can sometimes be mistaken, so they may give misleading information even when they try to tell the truth.

Furthermore, many witnesses in homicide investigations lie. Sometimes they want to conceal their involvement in the crime. Maybe they just don't want to be mixed up in the investigation. They may be afraid of repercussions if they testify against the killer. In many cases, especially in high-crime areas, people don't want to be viewed as a "snitch" for talking to the police. Investigators sometimes have difficulty finding witnesses who will admit to any knowledge of the homicide and agree to appear in court. Often homicide detectives will have to track down potential witnesses. In some states, the identities of witnesses are kept confidential to encourage them to cooperate.

Witness interviews and interrogations are not the same thing. A witness interview can resemble a question-and-answer session. The detective may try to make the witness as comfortable as possible and avoid making accusations. In an interrogation, detectives try to extract the truth from someone they believe has lied to them. The individual can be either a reluctant witness or a potential suspect. An interrogation is often held in a deliberately oppressive small room containing just a table and chairs.

Interviewers and interrogators may use psychological manipulation to get the full story from a subject. Detectives sometimes use their acting ability in playing a role. Fans of police dramas are probably familiar with the "good cop, bad cop" ploy in questioning a subject, but real interviewers and interrogators are more subtle. In the initial interview, detectives may try to develop a rapport with the subject and observe his or her reactions. Police may lie to a subject, such as by saying that he or she was implicated by evidence from the scene. They may appeal to the subject's conscience or make threats, such as raising the possibility that he or she could be held as an accessory after the fact. A subject may undergo a polygraph (lie detector) test, but the results are generally not admissible in court.

Establishing Guilt

Homicide cases can sometimes take years and thousands of hours of work before they are solved. The textbook *Introduction to Law Enforcement and Criminal Justice* lays out the elements of a successful criminal investigation:

- All physical evidence is collected and preserved properly
- Witnesses have been intelligently interviewed
- The suspect, if willing, has been effectively interrogated

Captain Michael DeMaio (*left*) and Lieutenant John Zutic of the Essex County Homicide Task Force compile a list of possible suspects involved in the Scheerer Avenue shooting and several related crimes. On the whiteboard, they have noted the classic informational questions: What Next? Who? Where? When?

- All leads are properly developed
- The investigation is reported properly

If these provisions have been fulfilled, the case is ready to be presented to the prosecutor.

Proper documentation of all aspects of the investigation is crucial for putting together a case that will hold up in court. Detectives take notes of every important development as well as mundane details. If a lead goes nowhere, for example, the detective makes a note. Otherwise he or she may be asked later about why the lead was neglected. Field notes are later incorporated into formal reports. Any mistakes made during the course of the investigation could impact a prosecutor's future case. If an officer makes a single error in the crime scene log, for example, a defense attorney could argue that his testimony is not reliable. It could cast doubt on the integrity of the crime scene.

It is also important that detectives take care to follow the laws and regulations when dealing with the suspect. Detectives are permitted to pressure witnesses in certain ways that are forbidden during an interrogation of a suspect. Accused suspects have legal rights that must be observed. These are summarized in the Miranda warning issued before interrogations:

You have the right to remain silent. Anything you say can and will be used against you in a court of law. You have the right to an attorney. If you cannot afford an attorney, one will be appointed for you. If you decide to answer questions, you have the right to stop at any time.

Suspects must be in police custody—usually, this means under arrest—for a Miranda warning to be necessary. In addition, detectives are forbidden from using coercion to obtain a confession. Suspects must be treated humanely. Interrogations are often videotaped to prove that detectives respected the suspect's legal rights.

A Los Angeles detective who was the chief investigator at the crime scene at Phil Spector's home displays a firearm belonging to Spector during the 2007 murder trial. Detectives help prosecutors with court materials and need to be meticulously prepared for their court testimonies.

Taking the Case to Court

Detectives on a case continue to play a role as the case is taken to trial. They are more familiar than anyone else with the evidence, witnesses, and sequence of events of the case. They help prepare the material that will be used in court.

The defendant may appear in court during several pretrial proceedings. At the initial appearance, for example, the judge informs the defendant of the charges and may set bail. Homicide suspects are rarely allowed out on bail, however.

Detectives must prepare thoroughly before testifying in court. The trial may take place months or years after the investigation was concluded. The detective should review all notes and reports relevant to the case. He or she should also meet with the prosecutor to discuss how the case will be presented. The detective should anticipate any questions from the defense attorney, who has access to all the evidence and reports related to the case. The defense may try to cast doubt on the detective's handling of the investigation, and the detective will need to defend his or her decisions. Even minor details may be brought up during cross-examination by the defense.

For the jury, testimony by detectives can be the deciding factor of the case. A detective who is well-prepared to discuss the case and professional in attitude and appearance is an asset for the prosecution.

CHAPTER FOUR

PREPARING FOR A LAW ENFORCEMENT CAREER

The job of homicide detective is a profound responsibility. When a life is lost to homicide, it is impossible to undo the hurt and damage of the act. Homicide detectives, however, can see that justice is done for the victim, the survivors, and the community. It's a demanding job, and the sensationalistic nature of some homicide cases can make the work even more challenging. On its Web site, the San Jose Police Department states:

Murder investigations are the most complex, sensitive and labor intensive investigations conducted by any law enforcement agency. No other type of case generates the same amount of public interest, has the same propensity to dominate the news media, or can propel once anonymous people to the national spotlight. Likewise, sensational murders can subject the investigating law enforcement agency to the intensive scrutiny of the lengthy judicial process, media analysts, and public opinion.

The job of homicide detective requires exceptional ability and dedication. But every homicide detective starts out as a patrol officer. Before asking yourself if you have what it takes to be a homicide detective, you need to step back and ponder whether a career in law enforcement is a good match for your personality, abilities, and goals.

Personal Qualities

People are sometimes attracted to law enforcement positions for the wrong reasons. They may be drawn to the idea of a homicide detective having a high-profile, action-packed job. Their interest in law enforcement might lay more in carrying a gun and ordering people around than preserving order and pursuing justice. Before seriously considering a career in law enforcement, a candidate should do a self-assessment and make sure that he or she is motivated by the right reasons. The law enforcement Code of Ethics, as established by the International Association of Chiefs of Police opens with the statement:

As a Law Enforcement Officer, my fundamental duty is to serve mankind; to safeguard lives and property; to protect the innocent against deception, the weak against oppression or intimidation, and the peaceful against violence or disorder; and to respect the Constitutional rights of all men to liberty, equality and justice.

An NYPD officer peers into a subway car due to a "credible threat" to the transit system. Any police officer must be prepared to deal with critical situations as well as routine duties.

Because law enforcement officers—and especially detectives—are charged with upholding the law, the consequences are greater when they violate the trust of the public by abusing their power or breaking laws.

Many police departments use the phrase "to protect and serve" as their motto, and the best law enforcement officers take the meaning of the words to heart. Police officers and detectives keep the community safe. They help people during extreme situations. But potential recruits should also recognize the challenges and drawbacks of police work. It can be dangerous. It can be thankless—the public tends to notice occasional bad behavior by the police more than everyday accomplishments. Police officers and detectives usually don't have a nine-to-five schedule. The stresses of the job sometimes take a toll on officers' family lives. The earnings are solid, but the private sector would pay more for the equivalent amount of work.

In his law enforcement career guide, renowned former FBI agent John Douglas lists several traits that are essential for successful officers or detectives. They need life experience and maturity. They need empathy. They need communication skills—written as well as verbal, listening as well as speaking, and for dealing with criminal and civilians as well as colleagues. They must be able to think clearly during a complicated investigation or during a crisis. They must also be able to exercise good judgment. Finally, they must have integrity, flexibility, respect for authority, and confidence.

An officer or detective must meet certain physical requirements. Applicants undergo a basic medical review that includes hearing and vision tests. Police departments require a certain level of fitness. The physical test generally includes a distance run, an obstacle course, weight lifting, sit-ups, push-ups, and pull-ups. Some departments have a minimum age of twenty-one and a maximum age of thirty-five or forty for joining the force.

A law enforcement candidate will undergo a strict background check. In general, a past felony conviction disqualifies someone from law enforcement. The background check and interview will yield information such as traffic violations, poor credit history, and drug use. None of these disqualify a

An applicant runs a police academy obstacle course. Training exercises test how well prospective officers can meet challenges that they may face in the field.

DIVERSITY ON THE FORCE

Police departments have long recognized the importance of having a diverse force that reflects a diverse population of residents. Diversity within the department helps build trust with communities. People are more likely to trust the police when they meet officers and detectives with whom they share a race, gender, ethnicity, or language.

Departments in large cities promote diversity through recruiting efforts. They place ads in ethnic newspapers. Recruitment officers visit immigrant communities. Forms ask applicants about proficiency in foreign languages. Many big cities, including New York and Los Angeles, have seen an increase in diversity since 2000.

In particular, women tend to be underrepresented in law enforcement. In the past, women on the force experienced sexism from colleagues. Irma Rivera, who entered the NYPD in 1982, described to DNAinfo.com how she'd hear "lewd comments" and "wisecracks about her weight when she became pregnant with her first child." Rivera worked her way up the ranks to become a homicide detective in Manhattan's South homicide squad. Today, such harassment of women would not be tolerated, according to former NYPD Deputy Chief Kathy Ryan, who was also quoted in the DNAinfo.com article: "Society has changed so much for women, and that includes the Police Department."

Nonetheless, women still make up less than 15 percent of officers among local police departments, according to the Bureau of Justice Statistics. In the NYPD, there's only about one woman on each homicide squad. Some departments try to reach out to women by holding women's recruitment and networking events.

candidate from being hired, but they do raise red flags to a potential employer. Too many red flags indicate a history of irresponsible behavior.

Education and Experience

A high school diploma is the minimum educational level required to join many police departments, but higher education can be an asset for a potential recruit. In particular, anyone hoping to eventually become a homicide detective should consider getting a degree. A college education supplies the candidate with specialized skills and knowledge, as well as critical thinking and communication skills. College students gain experience in interacting with people from diverse backgrounds. A two-year degree, a four-year degree, or a certain number of college credits can give an applicant an edge in the hiring process. Applicable majors include criminal justice and forensic science as well as computer science and accounting. Some departments consider fluency in a foreign language an asset, especially in departments in big multicultural cities. Military veterans are often given preferential status in hiring.

In some areas, recent high school graduates or even high school students with a passion for law enforcement may familiarize themselves with the field by enrolling in a cadet program. They can acquire valuable practical experience serving as a community services officer or similar title until they reach the minimum age to apply for a job as an officer. Often aspiring law enforcement officers then apply to the police force when they turn twenty-one. The requirements and duties of cadet programs vary from one department to another—some departments offer paid cadet positions. Other programs that involve civilian participation include law enforcement explorers, police reserve officers, and police auxiliary.

Some law enforcement agencies—on federal, state, and local levels—offer internship opportunities. These may provide a broad exposure to law enforcement duties or specialize in a certain subject area, such as crime analysis. Often the

An NYPD police instructor gives a lecture on gangs during a mandatory criminal investigation course for detectives. The 105-hour course is spread over 15 days.

positions require that applicants be full-time students. Departments may offer volunteer opportunities.

Previous job experience, even in unrelated fields, can provide skills that are valuable for a law enforcement career. People in customer service jobs, for example, have likely developed good communication skills. A glowing reference from a previous employer will show that the candidate has a good work ethic.

Police Academy

Before an officer steps out to patrol the streets, he or she must attend police academy. Some recruits complete the academy before finding a job, but most new officers are sent to the academy after they are hired. This training, which generally lasts from two to six months, will equip the officer with the knowledge, skills, and abilities necessary to perform the job.

Police academy is a rigorous and intensive course that combines classroom instruction with practical training. A recruit learns the laws that he or she will have to enforce, the protocol for writing reports, and investigative techniques. He or she spends time on the firing

This officer demonstrates handcuffing techniques during police academy training. Police recruits learn practical skills as well as police science, law, and social science.

range, learning about weapons, and in the gym, becoming proficient in self-defense, arrest techniques, and the appropriate use of force. The hours spent on vehicular operation are particularly valuable—more officers are killed in car accidents than are killed by criminals.

Small police departments generally send their trainees to regional or state academies. Large police departments operate their own academies. Officers in the New York Police Department, for example, are trained at the NYPD Academy run by the NYPD Training Bureau.

CHAPTER FIVE

JOINING THE FORCE

n 2009, retired NYPD homicide detective Michael Sapraicone responded to questions from *New York Times* readers. He weighed in on topics from dealing with victims' families ("Families react differently—some want justice and will cooperate, and some want to forget and will shy away.") to false confessions ("To avoid these confessions, the detective should check to see if the subject could have possibly committed the crime. The detective needs to confirm the details of the homicide but not reveal all."). He described one of the most bizarre motives for murder that he encountered during his career: a Pakistani resident of New York attempted to kill his sister and succeeded in killing her lover on the orders of his father, who lived back in Pakistan.

Sapraicone began his NYPD career as a transit officer—an officer who patrols subways and other mass transportation systems in the city. In his twenty years with the department, he spent ten as a homicide detective. Of his job, he said, "Some people do just fall into the job of investigator, but most

A transit officer looks into the window of a commuter train. Transit officers on patrol duty are responsible for the safety of passengers on trains and buses and in stations.

make it their career goal. I never wanted to be a police officer, only a detective."

Getting the Job

A career as a law enforcement officer and, eventually, a homicide detective, begins with filling out a job application for a police department. Many departments provide the forms online. A potential recruit should start early—the selection process for new recruits generally begins six months in advance of the start date for police academy. The specific sequence and requirements of the application process vary from one department to another, but the general elements are the same. Many police departments offer extensive information and preparation tips on their Web sites.

Next, the applicant must take a variety of tests and exams. The written aptitude test typically includes questions on reading, English usage, math, and police situations. It may include both multiple-choice questions and essay questions. Applicants should familiarize themselves with the format of the test, study for all topics well ahead of time, and arrive well-rested for the test.

The physical fitness test requires that applicants demonstrate their strength, agility, endurance, and aerobic capacity. The applicant should know the requirements and exercise regularly for months in advance. Some

High school students participate in a Junior ROTC Officer Candidate Course at Fort Campbell, Kentucky. Young adults interested in pursuing a career as a detective can choose from a variety of programs that provide hands-on experience.

TESTING INTO THE NYPD

The New York Police Department is one of the nation's most elite law enforcement forces. The NYPD Police Officer Entrance Exam assesses applicants' cognitive ability, observational skills, and mental acuity. Questions may test for abilities in written comprehension, written expression, memorization, problem sensitivity, deductive reasoning, inductive reasoning, information ordering, spatial orientation, and visualization. The exam is completed on a computer at a testing station in Manhattan or Brooklyn. Applicants must receive a score of 70 percent to pass.

Here is a sample question:

Reckless Endangerment—The crime of reckless endangerment is committed when a person performs an act, realizing that he is unjustifiably creating a great risk that one may be seriously injured or killed, and disregards the risk.

According to the definition given, which one of the following is the best example of reckless endangerment?

A. Al Green, an exterminator, sprays Bob Boyd's house with a powerful chemical insecticide as Boyd requested. Nobody is supposed to be in the house, since inhaling the chemical could cause death. Unknown to Green, one of Boyd's children is sleeping upstairs during the spraying.

B. Joe Brown, a trapeze artist, performs for a circus. As part of his act, he dangles from a rope 250 feet in the air without a safety net beneath him. There are no spectators seated nearby.

C. Bill White, a construction worker, is removing bricks from a foot bridge 30 feet above a highway. Since he has nothing in which to cart the bricks away, he decides to drop them down onto the highway, where he sees many autos passing below.

D. Jimmy Ocher, a teenager, receives a set of darts as a present. Because he has no dart-board, he throws his darts at the wall in his bedroom when no one else is home, realizing he could be causing serious damage to the property.

Answer: C

[Source: "New York City Police Department Police Officer Candidate Test Preparation Kit." Retrieved March 5, 2013 (http://www.nypd2.org/pdf/prepkitjan2005.pdf).]

departments offer training tips, including specific exercise regimens, to help applicants get into shape. It's a good idea to reach a higher fitness level than necessary because nerves can affect performance during the actual test.

Applicants tend to worry most about the physical requirements, but experts in the field emphasize the importance of the oral interview. The interview is the applicant's first chance to make a great personal impression on possible future coworkers. Before the interview, the applicants do some research on the department, learning information such as the organizational structure, the names of some top officers, the layout of the precincts, current issues of concern, details about the community served, and the duties of an entry-level job. They should practice answering questions ahead of time in mock interviews and prepare a brief closing statement. On the day of the interview, applicants should dress appropriately and arrive early. During the interview, the panel will ask questions that gauge whether they possesses the knowledge, skills, and abilities necessary for the job. These may cover personal history, hypothetical scenarios, and views on law enforcement. Applicants should consider each question carefully and avoid rushing into answers.

During the background investigation, investigators will check out records from the applicant's personal, financial, educational, and legal history. They may interview friends, family members, and former employers. The candidate is fingerprinted and may undergo a background interview.

Law enforcement applicants undergo a polygraph exam. An examiner monitors the result of a polygraph test on a computer. Polygraphs record vital signs such as blood pressure and breathing rate that tend to change when the test subject lies.

The psychological exam evaluates a candidate's psychological and emotional fitness for the job. It includes a written exam test and may require an interview with a psychologist.

The polygraph exam is administered by a trained polygraph examiner. Its purpose is to confirm background information.

The medical exam confirms that the applicant's physical health is sufficient for the job. Drug testing may be required.

On Patrol

For new patrol officers set on being promoted to detective, the time spent on patrol offers the opportunity to gain experience and learn the nuts-and-bolts work of policing. New officers begin with a probation period, usually lasting about a year. During this time, they undergo on-the-job (OTJ) training or field training alongside seasoned officers.

The patrol division is frequently described as the backbone of the police department. Patrol officers have the most direct contact with the community—they represent the arm of the law in the everyday life of citizens. When on duty, they are expected to prevent crime, apprehend criminals, and preserve the peace. They respond to dispatches from police headquarters as well as direct requests for help from the public. These may cover a huge range of situations. Patrol officers respond to reports of possible crimes and to circumstances such as accidents, emergencies, disturbances of the peace, reports of missing persons, and threats to public safety. Depending on the situation, they may have to make an arrest, issue a citation, mount a preliminary investigation, or redirect a complaint to a different authority. Patrol officers enforce parking and traffic regulations and respond to vehicular accidents. When necessary, they administer first aid. They provide crowd control at public events. They also address the day-to-day concerns of the public and support crime prevention efforts among the community.

Depending on the size of the department, ambitious young officers may be able to apply to various specialized units. According to Michael Sapraicone:

> The career path for becoming a detective varies. There are many units that you can enter that have an investigative track and will automatically promote you after eighteen months. The key is to establish yourself, and get into one of these units. It's the same as if you were applying for a new job: You need to request, be interviewed and be accepted.

After a few years on the job, a new officer will be able to take control of a contentious situation with confidence. He or she will be experienced in dealing with the public as an authority figure and be competent in managing a crime scene. The officer will be able to write clear and accurate reports. He or she will be familiar with the crime patterns in the city and will have dealt with a range of crimes. This knowledge and experience will prove invaluable on being promoted from officer to detective. According to Sapraicone, "Usually, detectives are the ones who keep pushing when others have had enough—that is what makes the difference."

Up for Promotion

The formal procedure for promotion to detective varies greatly from one police department to another. Generally, an officer completes a certain number of years—often two or three—as a patrol officer before becoming eligible for promotion. As mentioned by Sapraicone, promotions are automatic in some units after eighteen months. This policy is especially likely in investigative units. Applying to one of these units may entail some of the same requirements as the initial application to the force.

The department bases its decision on transfer or promotion on a number of factors. An officer must be highly recommended by a commanding officer. The process may require a job performance review, passing a detective's exam,

A police officer receives congratulations on being promoted to detective. A detective generally must gain extensive investigative experience before being assigned to the homicide division.

and an oral interview. Bureaucratic factors, such as an officer's place on a promotion list, may also affect chances of making detective.

There may be a probation period for a new detective just as for a new patrol officer. A promotion to detective may bring a pay raise, or it may be considered a lateral transfer that brings a new title but the same pay.

Detectives may take criminal investigative courses as they advance in their career. On-the-job experience is also an effective teacher. According to Sapraicone, "Most investigators really learn their trade on the job." A job with the homicide unit is a specialized and highly coveted position. New detectives often start out working in a precinct squad or investigating minor crimes. They can apply for a transfer to elite units such as homicide as they prove their abilities.

A promotion from officer to detective brings a new level of responsibility and a wider perspective. Sapraicone advises that beginning detectives cultivate patience and take care to follow every possible investigative lead in a case. "An arrest is not the answer unless the case is strong enough for a good prosecution," he says. "As a uniform or plainclothes officer, your tasks are to deter and arrest. To go from uniform or plainclothes [to detective], is very difficult sometimes because you are handling things right away."

CHAPTER SIX

BUILDING A CAREER

On December 3, 1957, in the small town of Sycamore, Illinois, two seven-year-old girls went outside after dinner to play in the first snowfall of the winter. A young man approached the pair and introduced himself as "Johnny." He asked one of the girls, Maria Ridulph, if she wanted a piggyback ride. The other girl, Kathy Signam, went back inside for a pair of mittens. When she returned, Maria and Johnny were gone. Maria was never seen alive again.

One of the people interviewed during the investigation was seventeen-year-old John Tessier, who lived a few blocks away from the two girls. Tessier had a solid alibi. A high school dropout, he was planning to enlist in the military. He said that he'd been out of town that day getting a physical exam in Chicago, Illinois. Shortly after Maria disappeared, Tessier left Sycamore to begin service in the air force. He eventually changed his name to Jack McCullough.

Maria's disappearance became a national news story. A thousand people searched the town and surrounding fields for her. Dozens of FBI agents searched for clues, but "Johnny" could not be identified. Maria's decomposed body was found five months later, in a forest 120 miles (193 km) away. The Tessier family had vacationed at a campground not far from the site.

The case went cold for decades. Then in 2008, McCullough's half-sister called the police. She said that years before, her dying mother had told her that McCullough had killed Maria.

Investigators reopened the case. Among the people they interviewed was the woman who had been McCullough's girlfriend at the time of Maria's disappearance. They asked her if she had a picture of McCullough. He had given her a framed photo shortly before he left. When she started to take the photo out of the frame, an unused train ticket to Chicago dropped out. It was for the day that Maria had vanished. The existence of the ticket contradicted McCullough's alibi for the day.

Detectives showed Kathy Sigman Chapman, Maria's friend who had also seen Johnny, a handful of photographs. She immediately picked out McCullough. Witness testimony emerged that cast doubt on McCullough's account of his actions on the day. Other witnesses mentioned multiple instances that McCullough had been accused of inappropriate conduct with young girls.

In 2011, Seattle homicide detectives arrested McCullough for murder, kidnapping, and abduction. The case went to trial in 2012, ending with McCullough's conviction and a sentence

Jack McCullough is escorted into the courthouse in 2012 during his murder trial for the 1957 death of seven-year-old Maria Ridulph. Ridulph's murder was the oldest cold case to result in a conviction and a sentence of life in prison.

of life in prison. Maria's murder is believed to be the oldest cold case to end with a conviction.

The Cold Case Homicide Unit

The cold case homicide unit is an investigative specialty that has been expanding in recent years. Homicide cases are not officially closed until they are solved, but some end in dead ends and frustration rather than arrest. Cases go cold when no leads remain that can be followed and detectives prioritize other urgent cases.

Technological advances, especially in DNA and fingerprinting, now give detectives means of analyzing evidence in cold cases that were not available during the original investigation. Running DNA tests on old samples can sometimes identify the suspect. If DNA was recovered during an investigation but never identified, the offender may someday commit another crime and have his or her DNA added to databases. When that happens, the DNA match with the cold case will automatically be identified. Computer databases can also reveal connections that were not apparent at the time, such as a homicide fitting in with a pattern of murders committed by a serial killer.

New investigative approaches can help crack cold cases. For example, detectives today spend more time researching the victim's background than was done in the past. Fresh evidence about the

A Portland, Oregon, cold case homicide investigator announces new leads in several cases dating back to the 1970s and 1980s. DNA evidence linked the murders to a serial killer.

INVESTIGATING GANG-RELATED HOMICIDES

A car pulls up to the sidewalk. A gunman shoots out the window of the vehicle at the people standing nearby within range. One or more victims fall to the ground and the car drives away. Maybe the victim was the object of a retaliation killing. Maybe a victim was just wearing the wrong color shirt in a neighborhood with high rates of gang-related activity. Or maybe it was just mistaken identity.

Gang-related homicides aren't easy for homicide detectives to solve. The shooter can often escape without leaving behind much evidence. Moreover, witnesses often prove uncooperative.

In some police departments, homicide detectives have improved their success rate for gang-related homicides by collaborating closely with other units and community groups such as antiviolence organizations. Detectives with the gang unit are familiar with the different gangs operating in an area and the rivalries between them. Community groups can sometimes persuade witnesses who are wary of the police to come forward. In addition, cold cases

may be reopened when a witness finally decides to cooperate and volunteer information about the incident.

victim in cold cases can open up new scenarios about the reason for the killing.

Some cold case squads routinely check on old files to see if any promising avenues of investigation have opened up. Just having an investigator new to the case, with a fresh perspective, can open up new possibilities. Other times, cold cases are revived in response to requests by families, new evidence from witnesses, or media attention.

When promising new leads emerge in a cold case, detectives investigate them using many of the same procedures as fresh cases. They gather evidence, interview witnesses, and review the crime scene, all while communicating with the prosecutor. Cold case investigators also refer to the original case records and contact the original investigator. They often appeal to the public for new information.

A cold case squad is usually somewhat independent of the regular homicide unit. Police departments generally don't allocate cold case squads a large budget or a large staff. A unit might consist of full-time detectives, forensic experts, part-time or reserve investigators, and volunteers with previous experience in law enforcement or criminal justice. Detectives from the regular homicide unit may also do some work on cold cases, either while on the job or during their own time.

Moving Up the Ladder

For many law enforcement officers, achieving the position of homicide detective is the culmination of a lifelong dream. Others, however, may aim for even higher levels of advancement. They can go about this in two ways. The first is by being assigned to a higher pay grade. A new detective may start at Detective 3rd grade and eventually reach Detective 2nd grade. (In some departments, the grades move in the opposite direction.) Exceptional service might merit a promotion to Detective 1st grade.

The other form of promotion is up the command structure to a higher class of job. This path means the detective would take on an administrative or supervisory role. The supervisory position above detective is sergeant—a sergeant in the homicide department would be a detective sergeant, rather than a uniformed sergeant. Homicide units ordinarily include both detectives and detective sergeants. The next rank up is typically the lieutenant, who would oversee an entire homicide unit. There are multiple grades for sergeants and lieutenants. Police captains manage divisions, which are made up of multiple units. Above police captains are the highest leadership positions in a police department, including commanders, deputy (or assistant) chiefs, the chief of police, and police commissioners.

Many police officers and detectives belong to unions or professional organizations. The largest police union is the Fraternal Order of Police. Unions bargain over pay and working conditions for their members during contract negotiations. They may also lobby government bodies and agencies over political issues relevant to law enforcement and provide resources to members.

Professional organizations give officers and detectives the opportunity to network and take advantage of professional training and support. The International Homicide Investigators Association, for example, aims to "provide active support to law enforcement death professionals through leadership, training, networking, and provision of resources and expertise to resolve cases." There are also many state-level homicide investigators associations.

In addition, detectives provide support to fellow law enforcement professionals in the department. Experienced homicide detectives often become mentors to younger investigators.

Maintaining a Balance

As a police officer moves up from patrol to detective to homicide detective, he or she will take on more duties, responsibilities, and stress. Law enforcement is a dangerous job. Even if a detective is never injured in the line of duty, he or she will have friends on the force who are. There will be close calls where death or injury seems like a real possibility. In addition, some difficult or tragic cases will stay on a detective's mind even after hours.

During this stage of life, a detective may also be establishing a household, raising a family, and taking on more

New York City Police Commissioner Ray Kelly holds a press conference on the 2010 car bomb attempt in Times Square. High-profile incidents, as well as everyday stress, add to the pressures of a police job.

responsibilities in his or her personal life. Balancing a law enforcement career and home life can be difficult in practical as well as psychological terms. A detective's job may require overtime, night and weekend work, and travel. Psychologically, the detective must approach his work with a different mental perspective than that of everyday civilian life. On the job, a detective must be assertive, vigilant, and ready to take control of a situation. At home, he or she must be willing to compromise, relax, and allow more emotional openness.

Law enforcement work can be notoriously stressful. A detective must develop strategies to cope with pressure, frustration, and violence encountered on the job. If he or she fails to deal with such issues, it can affect physical and mental health, as well as relationships with family and friends. In some cases, it can lead to domestic violence, divorce, substance abuse, and even suicide.

Many police departments offer resources for officers and their families, such as orientation for new recruits and counseling services. Detectives also need to take deliberate steps to manage stress. In general, it is important to maintain healthy habits such as a proper diet, a fitness routine, and getting plenty of sleep. Further, individuals must figure out what works best for them, whether it's talking to a therapist or just taking up a hobby. Keeping up a healthy lifestyle and a healthy view of life will be beneficial to work performance and a happy home life.

administrative Pertaining to management of the daily operations of an organization.

apprehend To arrest.

arson The crime of intentionally setting fire to a building or other property.

autopsy The examination and dissection of a body after death.

cadet A student training to become a law enforcement officer.

convict To find someone guilty of committing a crime.

crime lab A laboratory where physical evidence from criminal cases is examined and analyzed.

defendant Someone who has been accused of committing a crime.

felony A serious crime; specifically, a federal crime for which the punishment may be death or imprisonment for more than a year.

forensic science The application of science to the law.

homicide The killing of one human being by another.

manslaughter The unlawful killing of a human being without a premeditation or intention to kill or cause death.

personnel The people employed at an organization or place of work.

premeditated Thought out or planned beforehand.

probation The trial process or period in which a person's fitness for employment at a certain job is tested.

prosecutor The attorney who pursues legal action against someone or something in court on behalf of the government.

surveillance Close observation or monitoring, often of a person or group under suspicion.

suspect Someone who is believed to have committed a crime.

testify To state or declare under oath, usually in a court of law.

toxicology The branch of science concerned with the nature, effects, and detection of poisons.

victim Someone who has suffered injury or loss as a result of a crime.

warrant An authorization issued by a judge, such as to search for evidence or make an arrest.

witness Someone who has seen or can give firsthand evidence of a crime.

FOR MORE INFORMATION

Canadian Police Association (CPA)
141 Catherine Street, Suite 100
Ottawa, ON K2P 1C3
Canada
(613) 231-4168
Web site: http://www.cpa-acp.ca
The CPA is the national organization of Canadian police
    personnel.

Federal Bureau of Investigation (FBI)
FBI Headquarters
935 Pennsylvania Avenue NW
Washington, DC 20535-0001
(202) 324-3000
Web site: http://www.fbi.gov
The FBI is the agency charged with investigating a broad
    range of federal crimes.

International Association of Chiefs of Police (IAC)
515 North Washington Street
Alexandria, VA 22314
(703) 836-6767
Web site: http://www.theiacp.org
The IAC is the organization of police executives dedicated to
    providing global leadership in policing.

International Association of Women Police (IAWP)
12600 Kavanaugh Lane
Bowie, MD 20715
(301) 464-1402

Web site: http://www.iawp.org
The IAWP aims to strengthen, unite, and raise the profile of
women in criminal justice.

International Homicide Investigators Association (IHIA)
10711 Spotsylvania Avenue
Fredricksburg, VA 22408
(877) 843-4442)
Web site: http://www.ihia.org
The IHIA supports and assists law enforcement agences by
offering leadership, training, resources, and expertise in
solving cases.

Royal Canadian Mounted Police (RCMP)
RCMP National Headquarters
Headquarters Building
73 Leikin Drive
Ottawa, ON K1A 0R2
Canada
(613) 993-7267
Web site: http://www.rcmp-grc.gc.ca
The Royal Canadian Mounted Police is Canada's national
police service.

U.S. Department of Justice (DOJ)
950 Pennsylvania Avenue NW
Washington, DC 20530-0001
(202) 514-2000
Web site: http://www.justice.gov
The DOJ is the nation's primary federal criminal investigation
and enforcement agency.

U.S. Office of Occupational Statistics and Employment
Bureau of Labor Statistics (BLS)

Postal Square Building (PSB), Suite 2135
2 Massachusetts Avenue NE
Washington, DC 20211
(202) 691-5700
Web site: http://www.bls.gov
This is the nation's foremost source for career information,
    and where you can find the online *Occupational Outlook
    Handbook* (http://www.bls.gov/ooh).

Web Sites

Due to the changing nature of Internet links, Rosen
Publishing has developed an online list of Web sites related
to the subject of this book. This site is updated regularly.
Please use this link to access the list:

http://www.rosenlinks.com/LAW/Homic

FOR FURTHER READING

Dempsey, John S., and Linda S. Forst. *An Introduction to Policing*. 6th ed. Clifton Park, NY: Delmar Cengage Learning, 2011.

Dunn, William C. *Boot: An L.A.P.D. Officer's Rookie Year in South Central Los Angeles*. Bloomington, IN: iUniverse, 2008.

Ferguson Publishing. *Careers in Focus: Forensics*. New York, NY: Ferguson, 2010.

Foster, Raymond E., and Tracey Vasil Biscontini. *Police Officer Exam for Dummies*. Hoboken, NJ: Wiley Publishing, 2011.

Gilbert. James N. *Criminal Investigation*. 8th ed. Boston, MA: Prentice Hall, 2009.

Harr, J. Scott, and Kären M. Hess. *Careers in Criminal Justice and Related Fields: From Internship to Promotion*, 6th ed. Belmont, CA: Wadsworth Publishing, 2009.

Hess, Kären M., and Christine Hess Orthmann. *Management and Supervision in Law Enforcement*. 6th ed. Clifton Park, NY: Delmar Cengage Learning, 2011.

LearningExpress editors. *Becoming a Police Officer*. New York, NY: LearningExpress, 2009.

Rogers, June Werdlow. *Now Hiring: Criminal Justice Professionals*. Brule, WI: Cable Publishing, 2011.

Saferstein, Richard. *Forensic Science: From the Crime Scene to the Crime Lab*. 2nd ed. Boston, MA: Prentice Hall, 2012.

Samaha, Joel. *Criminal Procedure*. 8th ed. Belmont, CA: Wadsworth Publishing, 2011.

Schmalleger, Frank. *Criminal Justice Today: An Introductory Text for the 21st Century*. 11th ed. Boston, MA: Prentice Hall, 2010.

Schmalleger, Frank, and John L. Worrall. *Policing Today*. Boston, MA: Prentice Hall, 2009.

Schroeder, Donald J., and Frank A. Lombardo. *Police Officer Exam*. 8th ed. Hauppauge, NY: Barron's, 2009.

Siegel, Larry J., and John L. Worrall. *Introduction to Criminal Justice*. 13th ed. Belmont, CA: Wadsworth Publishing, 2011.

Simon, David. *Homicide: A Year on the Killing Streets*. New York, NY: Owl Books, 2006.

Swanson, Charles, Neil Chamelin, Leonard Territo, and Robert Taylor. *Criminal Investigation*. 11th ed. New York, NY: McGraw-Hill, 2011.

Sweetman, Timothy, and Adele Sweetman. *Investigating a Homicide Workbook*. Belmont, CA: Wadsworth Publishing, 2001.

Wallace, Harvey, and Cliff Roberson. *Principles of Criminal Law*. 5th ed. Boston, MA: Prentice Hall, 2011.

Young, Tina J., and P. J. Ortmeier. *Crime Scene Investigation: The Forensic Technician's Field Manual*. Boston, MA: Prentice Hall, 2010.

Allman, Toney. *The Homicide Detective*. Farmington Hills, MI: Lucent Books, 2010.

Branson, Jack, and Mary Branson. *Delayed Justice: Inside Stories from America's Best Cold Case Investigators*. Amherst, NY: Prometheus Books, 2011.

Bureau of Labor Statistics. "Occupational Outlook Handbook, 2012–2013 Edition: Police and Detectives." U.S. Department of Labor: Washington, DC, 2013. Retrieved February 15, 2013 (http://www.bls.gov/oco/ocos160.htm).

Di Ionno, Mark. "The Killing Cycle: Inside Story of the Essex County Homicide Squad as It Tries to Break the Murder Chain." *Star-Ledger*, August 14, 2011. Retrieved February 15, 2013 (http://www.nj.com/news/index.ssf/2011/08/essex_county_homicide_squad_in.html).

Douglas, John E. *John Douglas's Guide to Landing a Career in Law Enforcement*. New York, NY: McGraw-Hill, 2005.

Duke, Alan. "Phil Spector Gets 19 Years to Life for Murder of Actress." CNN, May 29, 2009. Retrieved February 15, 2013 (http://articles.cnn.com/2009-05-29/justice/spector.sentencing_1_judge-larry-paul-fidler-lana-clarkson-phil-spector?_s=PM:CRIME).

Echaore-McDavid, Susan. *Career Opportunities in Law Enforcement, Security, and Protective Services*. 2nd ed. New York, NY: Checkmark Books, 2006.

Kaplan Publishing. *John Douglas's Guide to the Police Officer Exams: Practical Tools to Help You Score Higher*. 4th ed. New York, NY: Kaplan Publishing, 2011.

Konkol, Mark. "Chicago Murder Clearance Rate Worst in More Than 2 Decades." DNAinfo.com, January 4, 2013. Retrieved February 15, 2013 (http://www.dnainfo.com

/chicago/20130104/chicago-citywide/chicago-murder
-clearance-rate-worst-more-than-two-decades).

Lambert, Stephen, and Debra Regan. *Great Jobs for
Criminal Justice Majors.* 2nd ed. New York, NY: McGraw-
Hill, 2007.

Los Angeles Times. "Complete Coverage of Spector's Trials."
2013. Retrieved February 15, 2013 (http://www.
latimes.com/news/local/la-me-spectorgallery,0,
5124683.storygallery).

Los Angeles Times. "In the News: Laci Peterson." 2013.
Retrieved February 15, 2013 (http://articles.latimes.
com/keyword/laci-peterson).

National Institute of Justice. "Death Investigation: A Guide
for the Scene Investigator, (Technical Update)." U.S.
Department of Justice, March 2010.

New York Times. "Answers About Investigating Homicides."
July, 2009. Retrieved February 15, 2013 (http://city-
room.blogs.nytimes.com/2009/07/08/answers-about-
investigating-homicides).

O'Neill, Ann. "Life Sentence Closes Oldest Cold Case." CNN,
December 11, 2012. Retrieved February 15, 2013
(http://www.cnn.com/2012/12/10/justice/oldest-
cold-case-sentencing).

Ortmeier, P. J. *Introduction to Law Enforcement and
Criminal Justice.* 2nd ed. Upper Saddle River, NJ:
Pearson Education, 2006.

People. "The Peterson Case: How They Got Scott." May 23,
2005. Retrieved February 15, 2013 (http://www.people.
com/people/archive/article/0,,20147640,00.html).

Pulizter.org. "The 2011 Pulitzer Prize Winners Local
Reporting—*Chicago Sun-Times*—Frank Main, Mark
Konkol, and John J. Kim." Retrieved February 15,
2013 (http://www.pulitzer.org/citation/2011-Local-
Reporting).

Ramsland, Katherine. "Murder Cop: A Profile of Vernon J. Geberth. *truTV*. Retrieved February 15, 2013 (http://www.trutv.com/library/crime/criminal_mind/forensics/vernon_geberth/index.html).

Ross, Winston. "Child-Murder Arrest After 53 Years." *Daily Beast*, August 6, 2011. Retrieved February 15, 2013 (http://www.thedailybeast.com/articles/2011/08/06/maria-ridulph-alleged-killer-arrested-how-cops-finally-found-jack-mccullough.html).

San Jose Police Department. "Behind the Scenes of an Investigation." June 20, 2012. Retrieved February 15, 2013 (http://www.sjpd.org/BOI/homicide/glimpse.html).

Weiss, Murray. "Retired Homicide Detective Recalls Her Own 'Prime Suspect' Drama." DNAinfo.com, November 21, 2011. Retrieved February 15, 2013 (http://www.dnainfo.com/new-york/20111121/manhattan/retired-homicide-detective-recalls-her-own-prime-suspect-drama).

INDEX

About the Author

Corona Brezina is an author who has written numerous books for young adults. Several of her previous books have also focused on issues related to criminal justice and the law, including *Amendments to the Constitution: The Fifth Amendment; Understanding Equal Rights; Frequently Asked Questions About Juvenile Detention; Careers in the Juvenile Justice System; Careers as a Medical Examiner*; and *Careers in Law Enforcement*. She lives in Chicago, Illinois.

Photo Credits

Cover Ivan Bliznetsov/Vetta/Getty Images; pp. 6–7 (background image) clearviewstock/Shutterstock.com; p. 7 © Jim Damaske/Tampa Bay Times/ZUMA Press; pp. 9, 26, 42, 60, 73, 86 iStockphoto/Thinkstock; pp. 10–11, 56 Aristide Economopoulos/The Star-Ledger; pp. 14–15, 22–23, 34–35, 39, 50, 52, 74–75, 81, 84, 90–91, 96–97 © AP Images; p. 16 © Mark Rightmire/The Orange County Register/ZUMA Press; pp. 20–21 Darren McCollester/Getty Images; pp. 28–29, 45, 58 Getty Images; p. 30–31 The Washington Post/Getty Images; p. 33 Jim Varney/Science Source; p. 43 Modesto Bee/McClatchy-Tribune/Getty Images; pp. 62–63, 70–71 Mario Tama/Getty Images; p. 65 The Washington Times/ZUMA Press; p. 69 © Bryan Smith/ZUMA Press; pp. 76–77 Chicago Tribune/McClatchy-Tribune/Getty Images; 88–89 Daily Chronicle, Kyle Bursaw/AP Images; cover and interior pages background textures Alex Gontar/Shutterstock.com, Eky Studio/Shutterstock.com, Andreas Liem/Shutterstock.com.

Designer: Michael Moy; Editor: Kathy Kuhtz Campbell; Photo Researcher: Karen Huang